WEAPONS AND EQUIPMENT OF THE GERMAN FALLSCHIRMTRUPPE 1935

A heavy machine-gun platoon moves into position immediately after landing.

ALEX BUCHNER

Schiffer Military History
Atglen, PA

SOURCES

Almann, Karl: Sprung in die Hölle, Pabel Verlag, Rastatt 1964.

Archive of the German Parachute Troops, Altenstadt.

Böhmler, Rudolf (revised edition by Werner Haupt): Fallschirmjäger (photo album), Podzun-Pallas Verlag 1971.

Buchner, Alex: Das Handbuch der deutschen Infanterie, Podzun-Pallas Verlag, Friedburg 1987.

Edwards, Roger: Deutsche Fallschirmjäger nd Luftlandetruppen 1936-1945, Stalling Verlag AG, Oldenburg and Hamburg 1976.

Gericke, Walter: Fallschirmjäger hier und da, Schuätz Verlag, Berlin 1968.

Götzl, Hermann: Kurt Student und seine Fallschirmjäger, Pabel Verlag, Rastatt 1980.

Hamann, Willi: Die 2. Fallschirmjägerdivision, Schild Verlag, Munich 1972.

Haupt, Werner: Fallschirmjäger 1939 bis 1945, Podzun-Pallas Verlag, Friedberg 1979.

Hove von, Alkmar: Achtung-Fallschirmspringer, Druffel Verlag, Berg 1954.

Kühn, Volkmar: Deutsche Fallschirmjäger im 2. Weltkrieg, Motorbuch Verlag, Stuttgart 1974.

Mergle, Albert: Geschichte und Zukunft der Luftlandetruppen, Rombach Verlag, Freiburg 1970.

Morzek, J.E.: Lautlos in den Kampf, Motorbuch Verlag, Stuttgart 1982.

Roon von, A.: Bildchronik der Fallschirmtruppe 1935-1945, Podzun-Pallas Verlag, Friedberg 1985.

Schmidt Herbert: Die Fallschirmjäger von Dombas, Schuütz Verlag, Berlin 1941.

Senger und Etterlin von, F.M.: Die deutschen Geschütze 1939-1945, J.F. Lehmanns Verlag, Munich 1960.

Tugwell, Maurice: Aus der Luft ins Gefecht, Motorbuch Verlag, Stuttgart 1974.

Parachute troops take possession of an important bridge with a light machine-gun providing covering fire.

Translated from the German by David Johnston.

Copyright © 1996 by Schiffer Publishing Ltd.

All rights reserved. No part of this work may be reproduced or used in any forms or by any means – graphic, electronic or mechanical, including photocopying or information storage and retrieval systems – without written permission from the copyright holder.

Printed in China.
ISBN: 0-88740-964-4

This book was originally published under the title,
Waffen Arsenal- Waffen und Ausrüstung der Deutschen Fallschrimtruppe 1935-1945
by Podzun-Pallas Verlag.

We are interested in hearing from authors with book ideas on related topics.

Published by Schiffer Publishing Ltd.
77 Lower Valley Road
Atglen, PA 19310
Please write for a free catalog.
This book may be purchased from the publisher.
Please include $2.95 postage.
Try your bookstore first.

THE GERMAN PARACHUTE TROOPS

Although the official designation Fallschirmjäger (paratrooper) already existed as the result of a decree by the Army High Command, military history acknowledges 29 November 1935 as the date of birth of the German parachute troops within the Luftwaffe. At that time Generaloberst Student, who was to be their leader, was not yet officially a member of the parachute troops. Nevertheless, he was already in command of the parachute school at Stendal. On 1 October 1937 he was named "Senior Aviation Commander IV." On 1 July 1938 he officially took over command of the German parachute troops as commander of the 7th Aviation Division (7. Fliegerdivision), a camouflage designation for the 1st Parachute Division) in Münster.

Only then did the planned formation of this new branch of the service and the development of clear operational principles begin. In addition to specialized selection and training of personnel, the force required weapons, equipment and transport aircraft suited to its unique role. Active in gliding since the nineteen-twenties, the general also gave consideration to the military use of gliders early on.

Student found an ardent supporter in his commander in chief Göring, who was quick to become enthusiastic about the new corps. For one thing, he saw to it that the army parachute battalion formed in early 1937 was taken over by the Luftwaffe at the end of 1938 and incorporated into Student's division. Proceeding parallel to this was the formation of divisional units. Parachute troops took part in a major parade for the first time in Berlin on 20 April 1939 (Hitler's fiftieth birthday) under the then Oberstleutnant Bräuer (1893-1947), who finished up the war with the rank of General der Fallschirmtruppe.

The training (the young soldiers were all volunteers, certified fit to become parachutists by the medical officer) was hard and multifaceted and the demands were very high. Jump training alone lasted six to eight weeks on average, with six parachute jumps, including one at night. The training was specifically aimed at producing a high-quality fighting man capable of independent action and from the outset was based on the concept of engaging a superior opponent under adverse conditions. For example, a paratrooper had to be capable of taking out a machine-gun nest or a bunker, even on his own and if need be armed with just his pistol and hand grenades. Consequently the comradeship and esprit de corps of this elite German force was unsurpassed.

The parachute troops played no significant part in the campaign against Poland in 1939. They remained in waiting positions and their primary role was that of guarding airfields and headquarters in the rear.

Hitler, Commander in Chief of the German Armed Forces, declared: "The parachute troops are too valuable to me. Therefore I will commit them only when it is worthwhile. The army has managed alone in Poland. I don't want to betray the secret of my new weapon prematurely."

The first successful parachute missions – during the Norwegian Campaign in 1940 to occupy important points and reinforce Battle Group Dietl at Narvik – were followed by the spectacular large-scale actions in the west in 1940, against Fort Eben Emael in Belgium and "Fortress Holland." These were followed in 1941 by the unsuccessful attempt to seize the bridge at Corinth and finally the full-scale parachute and airborne invasion of the island of Crete. Deeply affected by the heavy losses, after the fighting was over Hitler declared: "Crete has shown that the days of the parachute troops are over. The parachute troops are purely a weapon of surprise, the element of surprise has now been used up." Something strange now happened. Although only a few jump missions in at best regimental strength ensued, the German paratroop force grew more and more. By the end of the war, after the fiasco of the final and also the only night parachute action during the Ardennes offensive in the winter of 1944, it numbered a parachute army headquarters (formed in March 1944), two parachute corps (formed in January 1944), and ten parachute divisions. As well there was the Parachute-Panzer-Grenadier Division Hermann Göring. Of a total strength of approximately 200,000 men (150,000 in the summer of 1944), only about 15,000 were trained parachutists. Employed almost exclusively as ground troops after the Battle of Crete – in Russia, in Italy, in Western Europe, and even in Africa – the parachute troops proved themselves an elite everywhere they served.

In contrast, once the Allies had achieved air supremacy they used paratroops in growing numbers, ultimately carrying out the largest such operation of all time when, in the spring of 1945, 40,000 men descended on the Lower Rhine by parachute or glider.

ORGANIZATIONS

The actions in Belgium and Holland by the 7th Aviation Division together with the 22nd Airborne Division during the campaign in Western Europe in 1940 achieved surprising success and attracted worldwide attention. Subsequently, in the winter of 1940-41 the Luftwaffe High Command formed the XIth Aviation Corps as senior parachute unit. During airborne missions the air transport units were also placed under the command of the corps headquarters.

For the attack from the air on the island of Crete in May 1941 the XIth Aviation Corps under General der Flieger Student organized itself as follows:

Corps Headquarters
Corps units with
– Corps Reconnaissance Squadron

- XIth Transport Squadron
- Transport Company
- Airforce Signals Battalion with Radio and Field Telephone Company
- Parachute Anti-Aircraft Machine-Gun Battalion with 3 companies
- Parachute medical Battalion with 3 companies and airlanded hospital

Attached Units:
- Airborne Assault Regiment with 4 battalions
- 7th Aviation Division (Generalleutnant Süssmann with:
- 1st, 2nd and 3rd Parachute Regiments
- 7th Parachute Pioneer Battalion
- 7th Parachute Machine-Gun (Anti-Aircraft) Battalion (later a mortar battalion with 120-mm mortars)
- 7th Parachute Anti-Tank Battalion
- 7th Parachute Artillery Battalion (3 light batteries)
- 7th Parachute Medical Company
  (The 7th Aviation Division was renamed the 1st Parachute Division in May 1943)

  assigned as airborne troops under the corps' command:

  reinforced 5th Mountain Infantry Division (Generalleutnant Ringel).

This was the organization of the German parachute troops for their largest action.

A parachute regiment had three battalions of four parachute companies each. The 13th Company was a heavy company with eight heavy machine-guns and medium 81-mm (later heavy 120-mm) mortars.

Senior officers jumped too — Oberst Meindl photographed putting on his parachute.

Generaloberst Kurt Student, Commander in Chief of German parachute troops during the Second World War.

After the campaign in Western Europe in 1940 every 13th Company was armed with nine 100-mm Nebelwerfer (smoke-discharge mortars) and three single-shot 150-mm Do-Werfer (rocket launchers) in place of the heavy infantry guns. Also added was a 14th Anti-tank Company armed with six 37-mm anti-tank guns.

A parachute battalion was comprised of a headquarters with signals platoon and four companies. Parachute infantry companies consisted of three platoons of three squads (squad leader plus 12 men) each (compared to four squads in the infantry) with a total of eighteen light machine-guns (twelve in the infantry), three light mortars, and three anti-tank rifles. An alternate composition foresaw each battalion with only three parachute infantry companies and a 4th heavy company armed with eight heavy machine-guns and six medium mortars.

The composition of parachute units changed several times in the course of time. For example, for a time each parachute company had its own heavy machine-gun squad and a medium mortar squad with two heavy machine-guns and two 81-mm medium mortars respectively, in addition to its three platoons.

The Paratrooper's Badge — also referred to as the Parachutist's Badge — was one of the Luftwaffe's qualification badges and was not a war decoration. It was instituted through a decree issued by the Commander in Chief of the Luftwaffe on 5 November 1936. The de-

Oberst Sturm listens to a report following the jump at Corinth.

Having removed his parachute jump suit, Oberleutnant Becker issues combat orders to his company following the jump near Narvik by the 1st Battalion, 1st Parachute Regiment in 1940.

Paratroop officer in summer uniform with submachine-gun.

cree was proclaimed in Luftwaffe Official Gazette No. 1491, 1936, on Page 610. The conditions for the award of the badge followed on 10 May 1937 and a revised version appeared on 2 May 1944.

The badge consisted of a diving, gold-colored eagle inside an oxidized silver wreath, half of which was covered with laurel leaves (right side) and half with oak leaves (left side). The eagle grasped the national emblem (Swastika) of the former German Reich in its talons.

The badge was awarded for six practice jumps, including one night jump (parachute course), in the name of the Commander in Chief of the Luftwaffe, to officers and men of the parachute troops as well as to officials and members of the technical corps of the Luftwaffe who had received parachute training within the parachute divisions.

The badge was worn on the left breast of the uniform.

Since the shoulder straps with their badges of rank would be obscured by the parachute harness when the parachute jump suit was worn, special badges were introduced. These consisted of grey cloth patches with white wings and stripes and were worn on both upper arms. These were also worn on the flight suits of the aircraft crews.

The wings and stripes were white for officers and NCOs, yellow for generals. The background color generally corresponded to the color of the clothing – light or dark.

UNIFORMS AND JUMP CLOTHING

Like the alpine troops, the German parachute troops also had peculiarities and unique qualities concerning their organization, uniforms, equipment, armament, and training. The purpose of these was not to elevate them to the status of an elite force, rather they were necessary on account of their specialized role.

The standard service and dress uniform for parachute soldiers was that of the Luftwaffe, the branch of the armed forces to which they belonged. The situation was different regarding clothing for parachute jumping and combat on the ground. This parachute jump and combat uniform identified the "parachutists" as openly fighting soldiers and not – as was sometimes falsely claimed abroad at the beginning of the war – members of an irregular force, a so-called "fifth column" and so on.

The first item of equipment was the parachute helmet with the emblem of the Luftwaffe (an eagle) on its left side. It weighed approximately 1,000 grams, was round, without forehead and neck protection, with only a narrow helmet rim. Inside it was lined with a thin layer of foam rubber. A snug fit was guaranteed by a fork-shaped chin and neck strap which left the ears free. For use in action there were cloth covers, plain and camouflaged, with a wide band for attaching natural camouflage such as grass, twigs, etc.

In addition to the blue-gray flight jacket with yellow collar patches, Luftwaffe eagle on the right breast and the "Crete" cuff title introduced after the Crete operation, the parachute troops wore long field-grey pants which came to the tops of the boots. Worn over this uniform, which included a belt with the eagle on its buckle, was the parachute jump suit, which in the jargon of the troops was called the "bone sack."

The parachute jump suit was a waterproof, loose-fitting combat smock which extended to just above the knee and allowed complete freedom of movement. It bore the Luftwaffe eagle on the right breast, had a full-length zipper in front, zippered pockets on the both sides of the breast, and two large buttoned patch pockets at the upper thighs. The long sleeves were buttoned at the wrists. Initially in plain olive-green, after Crete the parachute jump suit was issued in a grey-brown camouflage fabric. After landing and removing the parachute and protective clothing, the belt and equipment were worn over the "bone sack."

The jump boots were made of stout leather, with medium-height shanks and thick, ridged rubber soles. Initially they were laced at the sides, but later (after Crete 1941) also at the front. Lined leather gloves with turnbacks were worn to prevent injuries during the jump.

Quilted, semi-circular knee protectors made of rubber and held in place by straps were worn at the knees over the trousers; cloth windings to protect the ankles completed the parachute jump outfit.

The entire uniform was extremely purposeful and proved itself in action; it later served as a model and example to the allies in every detail when they later formed their own force of parachute troops.

Whenever he parachuted into action, for example in the airborne operations in Holland in 1940 and Crete in 1941, every paratrooper carried the following necessary small items in his pockets: Energen or Dextro-Energen tablets, an energy-giving glucose preparation; an amphetamine drug, which kept the soldier awake (not a stimulant, however); large and small first-aid packets; handkerchief; matches; safety pins; string; thin wire; and nails, as well as a message pad with celluloid cover.

Oberjäger (non-commissioned officers) also carried a prismatic compass, binoculars and flashlight. In the breast pocket of the field jacket was a special identification card, and identity discs were worn around the neck. In contrast to the army soldiers, pay books were turned in by the units before takeoff and were not carried in action. Other items of equipment worn by the parachute soldiers: belt with carrying strap, a full canteen, entrenching tool and folding knife. The gas mask was carried in a cloth bag with zippered opening, later however it was dropped as an item of equipment.

The combat equipment employed by every parachute soldier on the ground – and which was dropped in containers – included weapons, rifle and machine-gun ammunition and hand grenades, as well as additional equipment assigned to individual soldiers such as flare

First public appearance by the new corps. Parachute troops in jump suits, part of the huge parade held in Berlin on 20 April 1939 to mark Adolf Hitler's fiftieth birthday.

March-past by paratroopers wearing parachute jump sits, armed with Kar 98K rifles.

The steel helmets worn by this group of paratroopers display the typical features of the design: a shallow rim with fork-shaped chin strap. None have cloth covers.

Paratroopers wearing "bone sacks" and armed with Kar 98K rifles and stick hand grenades; the soldier on the right has an MG 34 light machine-gun.

Paratroopers in spotted camouflaged jump suits seen after the jump into Crete. They have attached pull-straps to a weapons container. The third man from the right is still wearing his knee protectors.

Some of the paratroopers who landed on the Gran Sasso to rescue Mussolini, seen here with their light weapons: on the left a light machine-gun squad, fourth from left a man armed with a rifle with rifle grenade discharger cup, second to his left a paratrooper with a submachine-gun, then a rifleman.

pistols, wire cutters, claw hatchets, compass saws, illumination and signal flares, and various other types of arms and ammunition. Unlike the infantryman, the paratrooper did not carry his ammunition in the usual ammunition pouches, but in an ammunition belt of grey, olive-green or camouflage-pattern canvas which was worn about the neck. The belt was divided into twelve pockets which held a total of 120 rounds of 7.92-mm rifle ammunition (the infantryman carried 60 rounds in his ammunition pouches).

In addition to these arms and equipment there was the "assault pack." Used by all ranks, it was a field bag with attached tent square and was also dropped in containers. In the field bag were: knife, fork and spoon, rations for two days consisting of hardtack, various tinned meats and sausage, chocolate, biscuits, cookies, thirst-quenching tablets and cigarettes, as well as washing and shaving kit.

Flare pistols, colored smoke grenades, and air identification panels were used to maintain vital communication with the Luftwaffe and the air transport units.

LIGHT AND HEAVY WEAPONS

The weapons of the parachute troops did not differ significantly from those of the infantry apart from some minor modifications and exceptions.

When jumping into action each paratrooper carried only the 08 Pistol for self-defense, with two full magazines each with eight rounds in and next to the pistol, 10 reserve magazines and two pouches for machine-gun ammunition and several stick or egg hand grenades.

Based on the experience gained in Holland and Crete, after 1941 every paratrooper jumped with his main weapon – rifle, submachine-gun or light machine-gun. Members of machine-gun teams jumped with ammunition canisters so as to be able to go into battle immediately without depending on the weapons containers.

The stick-type hand grenade weighed 500 grams, had a delay of four seconds and a fragmentation effect up to a radius of 15-20 meters. Depending on the thrower, range was up to 25 meters. Not only could stick hand grenades be used individually; they could also be used in concert to form a concentrated charge for use against bunkers or an elongated charge against wire obstacles, etc. The stick hand grenade was usually stuck in the belt.

The egg-type hand grenade was simpler (no stick) and lighter (298 grams), but otherwise similar to the stick hand grenade. It could be carried comfortably in the pocket.

The Pistole 08 was an outstanding self-loading pistol with a caliber of 9 mm (pistol ammunition), an empty weight of 870 grams, favorable firing range of 25-50 meters, muzzle velocity of 320 m/sec, rate of fire of 10-20 shots per minute, and a magazine which held eight rounds.

The Kar 98K rifle was the standard weapon of the entire German Armed Forces and remained so until the end of the war. A clip-fed rifle (5 rounds per clip) with a caliber of 7.92 mm, it weighed 3.9 kg, had an effective firing range of 400-500 meters, a muzzle velocity of 755 m/sec, and – depending on the shooter – a rate of fire of up to 10 shots per minute. When equipped with a telescopic sight, the Kar 98K could also be used as a sharpshooter's rifle. A rifle grenade launcher which was introduced in 1942 (Schiessbecher, or rifle discharger-cup) allowed small 30-mm shells weighing 290-390 grams to be fired up to 250 meters by means of propelling cartridges.

The Fallschirmjägergewehr (FG) 42 was a version of a light infantry weapon developed specially for the parachute troops. It was for its time a highly advanced weapon and proved a success; however it was not introduced until 1943 and only entered quantity production in 1944. The FG 42 was an interim solution that embodied features of the automatic rifle and the light machine-gun and was capable of single or full-automatic fire. It had a folding bipod for better stability in action, a muzzle brake, a bayonet for close-quarters fighting which folded away beneath the barrel, and it could be equipped with a telescopic sight. Muzzle velocity was 761 m/sec, caliber 7.92 mm (sS, or standard ball ammunition), weight 4.82 kg, length 1 meter (1.11 meters with bayonet extended), sights 100 to 1,200 meters, rate of fire approximately 570 rounds per minute. Ammunition was fed from twenty-round magazines and each man had ammunition pouches for eight magazines.

The FG 42 entered mass production at a time when the assault rifle, a significantly better weapon, was reaching the troops in large numbers. Although the FG 42 proved to be a very effective weapon, no more than 4,400 were built (according to other sources only 524 in 1944).

Smoke grenades, smoke candles, signal and illumination flares, and concentrated charges completed the armament of the individual soldier.

Squad leaders were armed with the 9-mm Maschinenpistole 38. The submachine-gun weighed 4.3 kg and had an effective firing range of up to 200 meters, a muzzle velocity of 381 m/sec, and a rate of fire of 400-500 rounds per minute. Ammunition was fed from a 32-round magazine and soldiers armed with the weapon carried two longish canvas pouches, one on each side of his belt. Each pouch had three pockets, each of which held two magazines.

During a parachute jump the weapon was either slung in front of the chest, carried dismantled in the parachute jump suit, or packed with the ammunition pouches in the weapons containers. Armed with two MG 34 light machine-guns (augmented by the MG 42 from 1943) the thirteen-man squad (squad leader plus 12 men) possessed superior firepower to an infantry squad, which had only a single light machine-gun.

The MG 34 light machine-gun was an air-cooled, gas-pressure recoil-operated weapon designed for single or full-automatic fire.

The light machine-gun featured a folding bipod mount, caliber was 7.92 mm (the same as standard rifle

Left: Stick- and egg-type hand grenades.

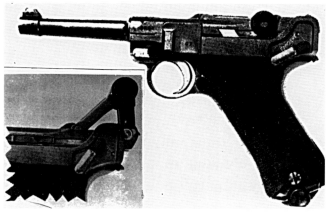

Above: Pistol 08 with toggle joint bolt mechanism.

Below: The new FG 42.

Paratrooper with Pistol 08 on his belt, into which he has stuck a stick hand grenade.

Parachute squad after the fighting in Belgium, armed and equipped with Kar 98K rifles, 08 pistols, stick hand grenades and ammunition pouches.

MP 38 submachine-gun with folded shoulder stock.

Left: A paratrooper lies in a muddy crater with his submachine-gun in firing position.

Right: A unit commander, armed with pistol and submachine-gun with extended shoulder stock, receives a report. In the center is an aerial delivery container.

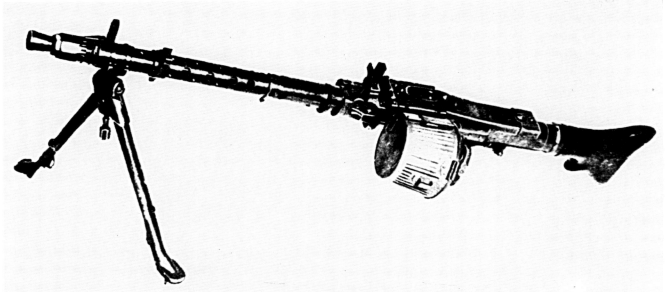

Above: MG 34 light machine-gun with bipod extended and ammunition drum in place.

Right: Light machine-gunner (foreground) and riflemen in combat.

Left: The crew of a light machine-gun (gunners 1 and 2) with the new MG 42.

Above: leichte Granatwerfer 36 light mortar.

Right: Loading the mortar with a 50-mm mortar shell.

The weapon with the greatest firepower —heavy machine-gun (here an MG 42) on a tripod mount with bipod extended.

Right: A machine-gun crew moves an MG 34 into position.

Left: A heavy machine-gun opens fire immediately after landing. The rest of the crew (ammunition carriers) approach after removing their parachutes (photo taken during training).

Heavy machine-gun in position in Crete.

Left: Heavy machine-gun firing on full-automatic. Note that the gunner is wearing a camouflage jump suit.

Gun crew changing the bolt mechanism of an MG 34.

The 81-mm heavy (later redesignated medium) mortar.

Mortar squad with disassembled mortar on the move after dropping into Sicily. Leading the way the squad commander; the second man carried the barrel, the third the bipod, the fourth the base plate, and so on.

Making a mortar ready to fire; note the mortar shell containers stacked next to the weapon.

Mortar crew with their short-barrelled mortar just prior to firing.

ammunition), weight 12.1 kg, effective firing range up to 1,500 meters, muzzle velocity 755 m/sec, and rate of fire 800-900 rounds per minute. Mounted on a tripod mount with firing mechanism and sight mount with aiming mechanism, the light machine-gun became a heavy machine-gun of the same caliber. Weight now totalled 33.2 kg, maximum firing range was 2,300 meters, optimum firing ranges 1,200-2,000 meters, muzzle velocity 920 m/sec, and rate of fire 900-1,000 rounds per minute. The weapon had a crew of three.

The high-angle weapons used by the parachute troops were almost the same as those used by the army. First there was the leichte Granatwerfer 36 light mortar, a muzzle-loader consisting of a smooth-bore barrel and a small base plate. The weapon was assembled when the crew went into position and was fired by means of a small firing lever. Caliber was 50 mm, total weight 14.5 kg, firing range 50-500 meters, range of elevation 42-85 degrees, range of azimuth 17 degrees left and right, muzzle velocity 75 m/sec, and rate of fire six rounds in 9-10 seconds. A crew of two serviced the mortar.

The heavy (later redesignated as a medium) mortar used by the parachute troops (the so-called Stummelwerfer, literally stub mortar) had a rather shorter barrel than the army version but otherwise all technical details were similar. The mortar had to be transported in three pieces – barrel (18.5 kg), base plate (18.3 kg) and bipod (18.9 kg). Firing was achieved by means of a bolt at the bottom end of the barrel, into which the loader slid armed mortar rounds from above. Caliber 81 mm, total weight 55.7 kg, firing range 60-2,200 meters, range of elevation 40-85 degrees, range of azimuth 9-15 degrees, muzzle velocity 75-174 m/sec (5th charge), rate of fire up to 14 rounds per minute, crew of three. Late 1943 also saw the introduction into service by the parachute troops of a new 120-mm mortar with a weight in firing position of 281 kg, a firing range of 6,000 meters and a crew of five.

The parachute troops did not have light and heavy infantry guns such as those used by the army.

THE SUPPORT UNITS

PARACHUTE ANTI-TANK BATTALION

In addition to the artillery, anti-tank defense posed a further problem, as suitable weapons could only be transported by air on a limited scale. Initially there was the simple anti-tank rifle as used by the army. It was operated by one man but soon proved to be ineffective against heavy tanks and the units were no longer equipped with it. Caliber was 7.92 mm (special ammunition), weight 12.7 kg, effective firing range less than 200 meters, muzzle velocity 1,210 m/sec, and rate of fire 10-12 rounds per minute. The weapon was capable of penetrating 30 millimeters of armor plate at 100 meters at an impact angle of 60 degrees.

A derivative of the schwere Panzerbüchse 41 heavy anti-tank rifle introduced by the army in 1942 was produced in order to give the parachute troops an anti-tank

Two-man team with a Panzerbüchse 39 anti-tank rifle in Holland in 1940.

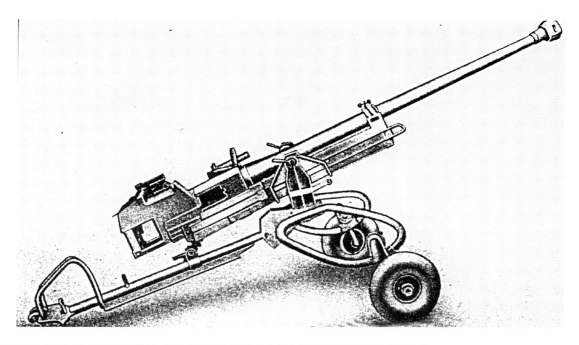

Right: Version of the Panzerbüchse 41 anti-tank rifle used by the parachute troops.

Above: 37-mm light anti-tank gun.

Well-camouflaged in an olive grove: a 37-mm anti-tank gun during the Battle of Crete.

A 37-mm anti-tank gun is loaded through the cargo hatch of a Ju 52 located in the right side of the aircraft.

A 37-mm anti-tank gun mounted externally beneath a Ju 52 prior to being air-dropped.

Right: A 37-mm light anti-tank gun descends beneath a quintuplet parachute.

Below: A 37-mm anti-tank gun behind a motorcycle-sidecar with the crew riding on and in the combination.

37-mm light anti-tank gun during the Battle of Crete.

weapon with which to replace the ineffective Panzerbüchse 38/39. It possessed the same conical barrel tapering from 28 mm to 20 mm at the muzzle with muzzle brake, but had a single-trail, light metal carriage with two small pneumatic rubber tires. Total weight, therefore, was only 118 kg (instead of the 229 kg of the army version). The anti-tank rifle, which broke down into five pieces, could be dropped beneath cargo parachutes. Range of traverse was 50 degrees, range of elevation -5 to +45 degrees, muzzle velocity of armor-piercing and high-explosive shells 1,400 m/sec, crew two. At the time of its introduction the Panzerbüchse 41 was an outstanding weapon with good penetrative ability – 55 mm of armor plate at 400 meters at an impact angle of 30 degrees – and a high rate of fire. Barrel wear was high, however, a barrel being good for only approximately 500 shots. Production, which was limited, was halted altogether after 1942.

Use of the 37-mm anti-tank gun posed a problem. The weapon was not capable of being disassembled and initially the 37-mm Pak was transported in one piece in a Ju 52 transport. Then the "packed" gun was carried externally beneath a Ju 52 and dropped beneath a newly-developed "quintuplet parachute." Developed in 1933/34, the 37-mm anti-tank gun was mounted on a split-trail carriage with large pressed wheels and pneumatic tires. The gun lacked a muzzle brake; however it did have an armor shield and a recoil brake with recuperator in the carriage. The 37-mm Pak was the standard weapon of the German anti-tank units in the early years of the war; by 1941, however, its unsatisfactory penetrative abilities meant that it was obsolescent. With a weight of 450 kg the 37-mm Pak had a range of traverse of 60 degrees, range of elevation of up to 25 degrees, rate of fire of 10-15 rounds per minute, muzzle velocity of 745 m/sec (HE) or 762 m/sec (AP), and a firing range of 7,200 meters. Following the parachute drop and the landing there was the difficulty of transport. Initially the gun's crew were only capable of moving the weapon and a few ammunition canisters by hand. Later on the weapon was attached to a 750cc motorcycle with sidecar, but this configuration could only transport four men and a quantity of ammunition. Finally there came 50-mm and 75-mm anti-tank guns with 20-ton prime movers, landed in large-capacity cargo gliders, as well as large numbers of Panzerfaust anti-tank weapons for most of the paratroops.

PARACHUTE PIONEER BATTALION

Since the battalion had no vehicles, but multifarious heavy equipment which first had to be delivered by air, its missions with mines and explosives extended to laying simple obstacles and mine barriers, demolitions, and supporting the parachute troops in the anti-tank role with mine barriers. An especially fearsome weapon was the flamethrower. Weighing 37 kilograms, it could be carried by one man. The flamethrower was capable of firing 35 bursts of flame, each of approximately 45 seconds duration, a distance of 25-30 meters.

Parachute pioneers photographed while laying a mine barrier (mines affixed to a board) in Italy, 1944.

Left: laying anti-tank mines.

The most feared weapon used by the parachute pioneers was the flamethrower (Battle of Crete 1941).

Left: A paratrooper in camouflage clothing with field telephone.

Right: Radio team with "Dora" set during the advance on the island of Crete.

Right: "Friedrich" radio team in action.

Left: An 80-Watt transmitter, used mainly for communications with the Luftwaffe.

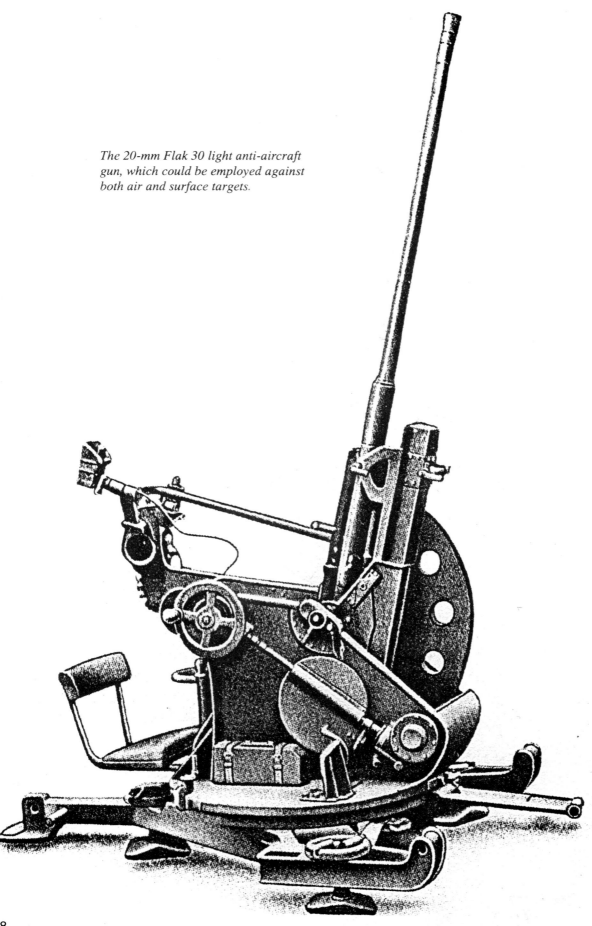

The 20-mm Flak 30 light anti-aircraft gun, which could be employed against both air and surface targets.

A unit medic renders first aid on the battlefield.

Enemy wounded were helped too — on Crete paratroopers transported wounded English soldiers to the aid stations.

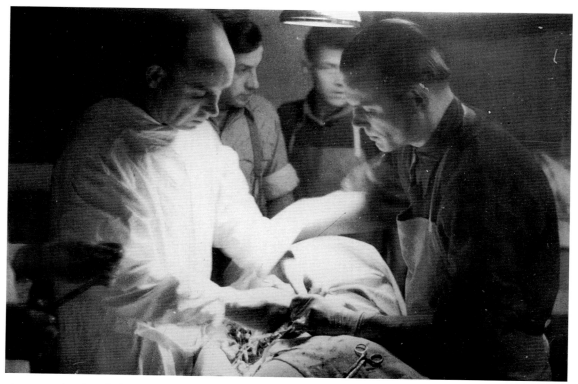

An operation in a field hospital.

Personnel load 750-cc BMW and Zündapp heavy motorcycle-sidecar combinations (B-Krad) aboard a Ju 52 prior to the airborne landings in Holland. As he will be landed by aircraft, the paratrooper (left) is not wearing a parachute. Instead he is wearing his full kit over his jump suit, with entrenching tool, bayonet, field bag, canteen, assault pack with mess kit, and tent square.

PARACHUTE ANTI-AIRCRAFT MACHINE-GUN BATTALION

As well as heavy machine-guns (Fla-MG 15 anti-aircraft machine-guns on motorcycle-sidecar combinations), the battalion also had the Flak 30 light anti-aircraft gun. This fully automatic, 20-mm recoil-operated weapon weighed 470 kilograms in firing position. The Flak 30's range of azimuth was 360 degrees, range of elevation -12 to +90 degrees. Firing range was 4,800 meters, ceiling 3,700 meters. Practical rate of fire was 120 rounds per minute; muzzle velocity was 900 meters per second with high-explosive ammunition and 800 meters per second with armor-piercing.

Mounted on a ground carriage and lacking an armor shield, the version of the Flak 30 for the parachute troops could be broken down into six pieces and transported over short distances.

The 20-mm flak was a capable weapon and could be used against air and surface targets alike. It was towed by a motorcycle-sidecar (B-Krad) on a single-axle cart with a load capacity of 400-500 kilograms. Each gun also included an ammunition cart. The crew rode on the two motorcycles. When first introduced into service the 20-mm Flak and its motorcycles could only be flown in by transport aircraft.

AIRFORCE SIGNALS UNIT

The parachute troops possessed inadequate communications capabilities. German industry had failed to develop capable lightweight radio sets. The Dora and Friedrich sets used by the parachute units were too large and heavy, and their performance was unsatisfactory. On the other hand, the state of development of field telephone communications was satisfactory. Communications by radio and field telephone were supplemented by runners and pyrotechnic signals. Air identification panels and signal flares were used to communicate with aircraft.

PARACHUTE MEDICAL COMPANY

Though fully air-transportable, once on the ground the company had no vehicles of any kind. Consequently any wounded paratrooper who could walk had to make his own way to the aid stations. The more seriously wounded could only be evacuated after a search of the battlefield following a cessation of fighting. All wounded had to wait until they could be evacuated by Ju 52 transports. The degree to which the medical personnel and doctors did their duty may be gauged by the example of Crete. Five doctors of the 7th Aviation Division were killed in action there, while in a rare case an Oberarzt (1st Lieutenant Medical) was awarded the Knight's Cross.

PARACHUTE ARTILLERY

Like any division-size unit the new parachute troops felt a need for their own artillery for large-scale actions. The sole question was the one of transporting the weapons to the battlefield. Since delivery by parachute was as yet impossible, the only option was to fly in the artillery by aircraft (Ju 52). At first the only artillery available to the parachute troops was the obsolescent Skoda Gebirgskanone 15, which had been designed as a gun for the alpine forces. The cannon had a box-trail gun carriage, wooden spoked wheels, a conspicuously short, thick barrel and an equally noticeably large armor shield. Maximum firing range was 6,650 meters. Total weight was 630 kg and the weapon could be broken down into seven components of 78 to 156 kilograms. A further problem was how to move the gun after landing, for which purpose the landing site itself first had to be secured.

Experiments with dogs as draft animals were a failure, therefore it was decided to use small Haflinger horses. The guns were fitted with paired wagon shafts for tandem teams. Stalls for the horses had to be installed in the aircraft. There were also light metal ramps over which the horses could be led onto and off the aircraft. The horses became used to air transport in a few weeks, and it was then possible to transport a horse-drawn battery to the battlefield by air, which happened in Holland in 1940. An eyewitness wrote: On 10 May a hail of English bombs began falling just as the air-landed artillery arrived south of Waalhaven. The Haflinger horses went wild, broke loose, and jumped out of the Ju's that had just landed. They raced about the field like mad, behind them the cursing and sweating drivers. And all this in the midst of an English air attack. Much time passed before the horses allowed themselves to be caught. It was the first and last air transport of horses by the Wehrmacht during the entire Second World War.

Use of the newly-introduced German Gebirgsgeschütz 36, which was the same 75-mm caliber, had a total weight of 750 kg and was transportable in eight loads, did nothing to reduce the demand for air transport.

Representing an entirely new weapon for use as artillery by the parachute troops were the so-called Leichtegeschütze, or light guns. These were in fact the first recoilless guns. They were designed to allow part of the powder gases to be directed to the rear through a large orifice. The rearward momentum of the gases equalled the forward momentum imparted to the shell, eliminating any recoil and allowing the barrel to remain stationary. Consequently, there was no requirement for a recoil buffer or recuperator. A typical feature of this type of weapon was a large cone-shaped orifice at the rear end of the barrel. Weight was minimized through considerable use of light metal. The light gun was thus deserving of its name, for it was possible to make it very light in weight, and it represented a complete departure from conventional gun design. On average its weight was 1/3 to 1/4 that of conventional guns of the same caliber.

The recoilless gun did not use rocket projectiles, rather it fired ammunition similar to that used by anti-tank guns.

The gun was developed by the Krupp Company and displayed all the qualities of the recoilless type weapon. The 75-mm Model 1 was the first of a series of designs. One special feature was a carriage with pneumatic rubber tires on spoke wheels with simple folding spars.

A subsequent development was the 75-mm Leichtgeschütz 40. Weight in firing position was 150 kg. Range of elevation was -15 to +45 degrees, range of azimuth 360 degrees. Muzzle velocity was 365 m/sec, and maximum firing range was 6,800 meters. Rate of fire was eight rounds per minute and the high-explosive shells

The standard artillery piece of the parachute troops in 1940 was still the Gebirgskanone 15 mountain gun manufactured by Skoda.

The standard artillery piece of the parachute troops in 1940 was still the Gebirgskanone 15 mountain gun manufactured by Skoda.

The first weapon suitable for the artillery role to be received by the parachute troops was the 75-mm Leichtgeshütz recoilless gun with spoked wheels.

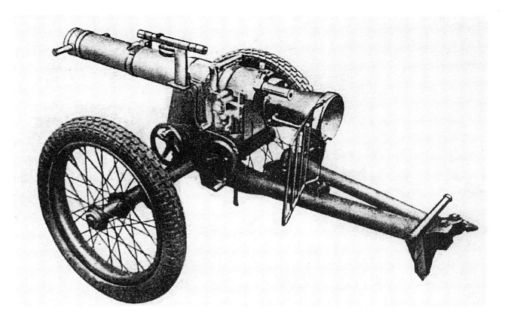

A further development of the 75-mm recoilless gun with wheeled carriage and shield.

75-mm recoilless gun on tripod mount.

The crew of a 105-mm recoilless gun during firing, Crete 1941.

Sentry with garrison cap beside a 105-mm recoilless gun in Sicily.

it fired weighed 5.7 kg. The gun's crew consisted of two or three men.

The weapon was mounted on a folding tripod carriage (one leg forward, two back) with small cast steel wheels which were removed when the gun was in firing position. Most lacked an armor shield, though some had this feature. Broken down into four components, the weapon could be dropped by parachute. Placed in service from 1940, it first saw action in the airborne invasion of Crete, where an air-dropped battery of four guns was committed. A five-kilogram hollow-charge shell was introduced later for the anti-tank role.

Later versions were intended to be broken down into only two loads, which were dropped packed in wicker baskets.

As the caliber of 75 mm proved unsatisfactory, there followed the 105-mm Leichtgeschütz 43. It weighed 485 kilograms in firing position, 515 in travelling position. Range of elevation was -15 to +20 degrees, range of azimuth up to 360 degrees. Muzzle velocity was 335 m/sec, maximum firing range 7,000 meters. At 14.8 kilograms, the projectile weighed the same as that of the lFH 18 105-mm light field howitzer. The gun crew consisted of three men. Like the 75-mm gun, the 105-mm light gun was mounted on a tripod carriage with large, rubber-tired wheels (also small wheels, from which the gun could be fired), with or without a protective shield. The rubber-tired spoked wheels were dropped separate from the rest of the gun, unpacked, beneath simple parachutes. Introduced in 1943, for delivery by parachute the gun could be broken down into five components weighing from 124 to 189 kilograms with aerial delivery container. Once assembled on the ground, the weapon could be pulled by two to three men or by a likewise air-dropped B-Krad.

Several improved types were followed by the LG 43, a recoilless gun with a caliber of 105 millimeters which could fire 6-7 rounds per minute to a distance of 8,000 meters. The two disc wheels were raised off the ground when the trails were spread, making all-round fire possible. A special locking mechanism held the barrel fast when in travelling position. The gun had a large upper shield with lower shield. Weighing 523.7 kg, it could be broken down into ten components, with the heaviest, the barrel, weighing 135 kg and the lightest, the sight mount, 7.5 kilograms.

A total of 653 75-mm and 528 105-mm light guns were delivered, and they later saw service with other combat elements in difficult terrain (alpine units, etc.). Though the recoilless guns proved a success they did possess some disadvantages, for example the stream of powder gas which exited the rear of the gun with its conspicuous cloud of smoke, the large flame from the exit nozzle, and the dust and dirt stirred up when the gun was fired, all of which endangered the gun crew and made concealment impossible. Furthermore, there were some difficulties involved in the manufacture of the special cartridges. Production was halted after the summer of 1944 as powder consumption was considered too high.

Not to be overlooked were the missions flown by the Luftwaffe as "flying artillery" in support of the parachute troops.

PARACHUTES

The life of the jumper depended on the careful packing of his parachute. On principle, therefore, each parachutist had to pack his own parachute. As per regulations this was done by two people: "packer and helper" worked together. Several years of tests and experiments at the Parachute Test Station at Stendal resulted in the

Parachute troops climb into a Ju 52 through the door in the left side of the aircraft.

The seconds before the jump.

A paratrooper dives out of the aircraft headfirst; the static line has not yet opened the parachute.

The various phases of parachute deployment during the jump.

Left: Parachutist seconds before the landing.

Below: Difficult landing maneuver with fully-blown parachute in gusty winds, Narvik 1940.

Recovering parachutes, some of which are still white in color, during the Crete operation.

Left: Parachute troops land in waves on Crete in 1941; note the camouflage parachutes.

Important signal to one's own airforce, the laying out of air identification panels: we are here! (Sicily 1943).

development of a reliable parachute for military purposes based on the safety chute used in civil aviation; this was the parachute in use by the parachute troops when war broke out. Designated the RZ 1 (back parachute with automatic deployment), it was a semi-circular cap parachute with 28 sections, a diameter of 8.5 meters (in plan section), and a surface area of 56 square meters. Maximum rate of descent, depending on the weight of the jumper, was 3-6 meters per second. With a jump height of 100 meters the parachute opened automatically after a fall of approximately 30 meters. The parachute was folded inside a parachute bag and was deployed automatically by a static line. There was no reserve parachute. An uncomfortable characteristic of the RZ 1 was its tendency to swing badly in gusty conditions, in addition to which it had a rather high sink rate.

An important part of the parachute was the harness, from which the jumper had to extricate himself quickly after landing. When putting on the parachute over the "bone sack" the wide parachute harness was locked firmly by four fasteners. There were two rifle hooks on the thigh straps and a snap fastener on one breast and one belly strap. In this way the harness was prevented from releasing itself during the jump. While the resulting level of safety was welcomed, the difficulty faced by the jumper in quickly freeing himself from the parachute after landing was not. Since absolutely calm wind conditions could not be counted on, the jumper had to expect to be dragged over the ground by the canopy – which in the wind acted as a sail – before he was able to open his harness and free himself from the parachute.

The RZ 1 remained in use until early 1940. Then followed the new RZ 16 with improved packing of the static line. The subsequent RZ 20 featured improvements in the central opening mechanism. It was first used at Crete in 1941 and remained in service until mid-1943.

The newly-developed central harness buckle, which enabled the parachutist to more quickly release himself from his harness and thus the parachute, was first used in limited numbers during the Crete operation.

Also developed in the course of the war was the RZ 36, the first triangular parachute and based on the Russian example. It had the threefold advantage of a mild deployment shock, little tendency to swing, and a softer landing. Dipl.Ing. Schauenburg submitted this parachute for patent on 6 May 1943; however it was never used by the troops in action. 1944 saw the introduction of a ribbon-type parachute. Approximately 120,000 parachutes were kept constantly in storage in a central location and could be issued as required. A sufficient quantity of cargo parachutes was also kept available.

The largest cargo parachute was the so-called "quintuplet." Designed in early 1940, it was five parachutes connected together and packed in one bag. Use of this system allowed 37-mm anti-tank guns, recoilless guns and motorcycle-sidecars to be air-dropped.

All parachutes were white initially, but by 1941 experience had shown that a white parachute was too conspicuous when lying on the ground and could be seen from a distance by the enemy. As a result parachutes in camouflage colors were introduced. Officers used parachutes with white caps which served as identifying markings.

AERIAL DELIVERY CONTAINERS

The parachute troops' most vital piece of equipment was the aerial delivery container, in which were placed arms, ammunition, other weapons and equipment. These elongated, box-shaped metal containers (there was only one model until Crete) varied in size and weight. A standard weapons container was 1.5 meters long, had a diameter of 40 cm, and weighed 20 to 30 kg empty and up to 130 kg fully packed. (Further stronger and larger containers of 500 and 1,000 kg were developed after Crete.) The interior of the container was padded to absorb the shock of landing and the contents were secured by leather straps to prevent damage. A special protective inner liner was also used when only weapons were packed. Sensitive radio and telephone equipment was installed in the containers with felt pads to protect against damage. Aluminum shock absorbers were screwed onto the bottom ends of the containers; these compressed on landing and thus reduced the force of the impact. The impact-absorbing caps were replaced if the container was to be reused. Two carrying handles were installed on each side of the container; as well, inside the container were two small, rubber-tired wheels and a light tow bar which could be attached after landing. These made the container easier to move and more mobile. In this way, two or three containers were often pulled and pushed one behind the other to platoon and company assembly points after landing. The use of various bright colors identified the contents of the containers and made them easier to locate in terrain. Colored smoke cartridges attached to the containers (red, violet, etc.) helped more quickly locate the containers and determine their contents. White rings and other markings painted on the upper ends of the containers identified the units to which they belonged. The weapons containers were released from the bomb cells of Ju 52 transport aircraft with each squad of parachutists. The Ju 52s flew in groups of three; the aircraft on the left and right dropped the parachutists and the one in the middle the aerial delivery containers. A standard parachute was installed on the end of the container and was deployed in the usual way by a static line. Depending on the size and weight of the load – which could also be pushed through the doors in the side of the aircraft – several cargo parachutes might be necessary. A squad of twelve parachutists required four containers, a platoon of forty to fifty men fourteen, to deliver the firearms, other weapons and equipment needed for combat. In addition to assembling the men, finding, recovering and emptying the containers quickly was a condition for the rapid attainment of battle readiness by the unit. Critical and dangerous situations could arise

Above: Cargo parachutes (weapons containers) swing earthward.

Right: An initial model weapons container is emptied; the markings are plainly visible (Narvik 1940).

Paratroopers remove their weapons from a container (Corinth 1941).

On the ground, weapons containers with their transport wheels in place are collected for subsequent use.

if, for example, the jump was made into the midst of the enemy and the paratroopers were unable to reach their weapons containers immediately.

Following the Battle of Crete, aerial supply containers were developed which, weighing 200 kg, could accept loads of up to 300 kg. Containers larger than 100 kilograms had to be carried beneath the fuselages of transport aircraft. In this regard it may be interesting to note that twice the required number of rifles, submachine-guns and light machine-guns were provided the parachutists, on the one hand to increase their fighting potential and on the other because of the possible loss of containers which were destroyed or could not be found.

Practical solutions to the problem of dropping heavy equipment were rather late in coming – after the large-scale parachute operations in Holland and Crete. Heavy loads such as anti-tank guns or motorcycle-sidecar combinations were packed in metal frames and, suspended on the underside of the transport or pushed out through the loading hatch, were dropped on a cluster of five "quintuplet" parachutes. Only a handful 20-mm anti-tank guns and a few anti-tank and recoilless guns were air-dropped into Crete.

TRANSPORT AIRCRAFT

The standard transport aircraft was the Ju 52, which had served satisfactorily with the German airline Lufthansa since 1930 and which the paratroopers called "good old auntie Ju." It was a cantilever low-wing monoplane of all-metal construction, which in this case meant corrugated aluminum panels over a steel tube frame, which resulted in an immensely strong airframe. The aircraft was powered by three BMW air-cooled radial engines each producing 830 HP. Maximum speed was 290 kph, gross weight 11 tons, and cargo capacity was approximately 17 cubic meters, or 1.5 tons or 12 parachutists plus jumpmaster and observer. Radius of action was 560 kilometers, while the crew consisted of four and later three men. Jumpers entered the cargo area through a door on the left side of the aircraft; loading of large pieces of equipment was through a cargo door on the right. The undercarriage was non-retractable. A Ju 52 normally towed a single glider but was capable of towing three DFS 230s.

The Ju 52 was an absolutely safe aircraft which could maintain height and course even with flak damage and the loss of one engine. The aircraft was also capable of taking off from unpaved runways and could if necessary land on roads and even fields.

Disadvantages included the aircraft's low speed, which almost made it appear sluggish, and its lack of bulletproof fuel tanks. As well its defensive armament was totally inadequate, consisting of an open revolving turret on top of the fuselage with a 13-mm machine-gun, and two 7.9-mm machine-guns firing from the fuselage windows.

GLIDERS AND CARGO GLIDERS

When discussing the subject of cargo- and troop-carrying gliders it is important to differentiate between the light gliders which were used solely to deliver parachute troops and the types outlined here which were also used to deliver other troops and supplies.

Three types of cargo- and troop-carrying glider were developed by the Luftwaffe before and during the war: the DFS 230 (light Class A), Go 242 (medium Class B), and the Me 321 (heavy Class C).

All three types of glider were simply designed and inexpensive to build. The DFS 230 (DFS = Deutsches Forschungsinstitut für Segelflug, or German Institute for Gliding Flight) was the only glider type in service when the war broke out and was considered an especially top-secret part of the parachute forces.

The use of gliders offered special advantages. With them an entire squad could be landed together from the air in a small area and once on the ground was immediately ready for action with its weapons with no lengthy forming-up. Parachute troops, on the other hand, landed scattered over an area 150-200 meters long and then needed a certain amount of time to collect their weapons and assemble. Since the tug aircraft released the gliders up to twelve kilometers from their targets, they could approach silently and land noiselessly directly on the target. Command of the airspace by one's own air force was a requirement, however, for the weakly armed transport aircraft with their unarmed gliders would be easy prey for enemy aircraft, resulting in the loss of the entire squad. The weather also played a large role and could be a disadvantage. The smoothest possible flight was desirable, as the gliders were prone to "dance" in windy conditions and frequently the tow cables snapped.

Classed as a light glider, the DFS 230 entered production in late 1939. It was of particularly light construction and consisted of a fuselage framework of light metal tube covered with plywood and linen. There was a glazed cockpit for the crew and behind it a compartment in which the soldiers sat one behind the other on a sort of seating beam. The wings were attached to the top of the fuselage in order to achieve a better gliding capability. The glider possessed an undercarriage with two small wheels beneath the fuselage for towing purposes and this could be retained or dropped. As a rule takeoff was in groups of three. For landing there was a simple, ski-shaped, sprung plywood skid beneath the nose of the aircraft, which absorbed the shock of landing and brought the glider to a stop. The DFS 230 weighed 820 kilograms (1.1 tons). Length was 11.24 meters, wingspan 21.98 meters and height 2.74 meters. The DFS 230 was flown by one pilot and could transport ten men with their small arms and ammunition or a load of 900 kg. The glider was simple to fly, capable of being flown at night and was easy to land.

The most commonly-used tug aircraft was the Ju 52, however the He 111, Me 110, Do 17 and Ju 87 were also used. Steel cables of various lengths and gauges were

A Staffel of Ju 52s on a stubble field in Holland in 1940. Note the open door on the left side of the nearest machine and the dorsal machine-gun position.

Right: A trio of Ju 52s taking off from an open field.

The aircraft began disgorging the paratroopers.

used to tow the various types of glider. Two (Tandem-Schlepp) or even three (Troika-Schlepp) DFS 230 gliders could be towed by the Ju 52, though this was only rarely the case. Usually the tug aircraft had only a single glider in tow. The DFS 230 was light enough so that it could be towed by even a light communications aircraft such as the Hs 126.

Maximum speed while under tow with a steel cable of 40-80 meters length was 185 kph. The attack gliders descended in a spiral dive from a height of approximately 1,000 meters at a speed of about 125 kph, finally arriving over the target in a 290-kilometer-per-hour dive. Beginning in 1941, the gliders were equipped with a braking parachute (which was deployed below a height of 50

The DFS 230 combat glider; the angle of attack suggests that the aircraft is in gliding flight.

Production of the DFS 331 combat glider was limited to a single prototype.

meters) for special "pinpoint landings." Use of the chute reduced the landing run to between 25 and 50 meters. As well, a braking rocket was later installed in the nose of the aircraft, further reducing the landing distance. As a final measure to minimize landing distance the skid was wrapped in barbed wire.

In action each company required nine gliders. In the operations in Western Europe in 1940, for example, Sturmabteilung (Assault Battalion) Koch (11 officers, 427 men, including 42 pilots) flew in forty-two glider-tug combinations each consisting of one Ju 52 and one DFS 230.

A total of 150 gliders were built by 1940, 1,022 by 1941, and by 1942 1,477 gliders had been delivered to the Luftwaffe's glider command.

Brief mention should be made of the Go 242 twin-boom glider, which was capable of transporting 23-25 men or 5.5 tons of cargo. With the exception of the transport by air of the 1st Parachute Division from Southern France to Sicily in July 1943, the Go 242 did not go into

A DFS 230 glider with landing skid and twin-wheeled undercarriage. The aircraft has a light machine-gun for self-defense, a feature rarely seen. The Ju 87 tug is visible in the lower left corner of the photo.

Go 242 twin-boom glider under tow by a transport aircraft.

action with parachute troops.

The Me 321 Gigant large-capacity glider was capable of carrying eighteen tons and could transport ninety fully-equipped troops or a 150-mm field howitzer and prime mover. The Me 323 was a powered version of the Me 321 with six air-cooled radial engines. Neither type was used by the parachute troops.

In the course of the war 3,000 assault and troop- and cargo-carrying gliders were lost: wrecked, burnt or destroyed by their owners.

Paratroopers leave a glider and move into action (Gran Sasso operation 1943).

Paratroopers attack after leaving a glider (training exercise).

A Stuka dive-bomber — friend of the parachute troops.